HQ
755.8
.Y44
1988

Yellin, Alan.

When your child
grows up too fast

$5.75

When Your Child Grows Up Too Fast

Alan Yellin, Ph.D.,
and Penelope B. Grenoble, Ph.D.

CB

CONTEMPORARY
BOOKS

CHICAGO · NEW YORK

Copyright © 1988 by RGA Publishing Group, Inc.
All rights reserved
Published by Contemporary Books, Inc.
180 North Michigan Avenue, Chicago, Illinois 60601
Manufactured in the United States of America
Library of Congress Catalog Card Number: 88-11855
International Standard Book Number: 0-8092-4669-4

Published simultaneously in Canada by Beaverbooks, Ltd.
195 Allstate Parkway, Valleywood Business Park
Markham, Ontario L3R 4T8 Canada

ACKNOWLEDGMENT

Special thanks to Charlene Solomon, who worked on the original research for this book.

—PBG

CONTENTS

An Introduction to *ParentBooks That Work*

It has been said that twenty-five-dollar words can be used to cover up twenty-five-cent ideas. In our increasingly technological society, jargon and complex language often confuse the meaning of information. This is particularly the case in the social and psychological sciences.

The "hard sciences" such as physics, chemistry, and biology have an advantage: there is little chance, for example, that a photon or a quark will be confused with something else.

In the human sciences, however, we have at least two problems with language. One is that the popular definition of a word such as *sex* or *intelligence* can differ considerably from the way a professional in the field might use it. Although we parents share a common pool of language with social scientists and teachers and therapists, words like *input* and *reinforcement*, *expectations* and *assessment*, mean one thing to parents and another to social science experts. Thus the danger that we will not understand each other is very real.

The human sciences' other language problem is jargon. A particular group of human scientists may develop obscure or seemingly incomprehensible language as a shortcut to communication among its members. Thus, jargon can be a roadblock when the experts try to talk to people outside their field.

The books in this series are the result of skillful collaboration between trained psychologists experienced in family and child development and a seasoned writer. The authors have strived to take twenty-five-dollar ideas and deliver them in language that is clear, concise, and most useful to you. In these six books, the emphasis is on presenting intelligent and practical ideas that you can use to help solve the age-old problems of child rearing.

This brings us to the very reason for these books. It might have occurred to you to ask, "Why should I rely on so-called experts when I can fall back on tradition and conventional wisdom? After all, the human race has survived well on what parents have taught children through the ages." Think about that for a moment. In the long history of human life on this planet, most of our energy has been spent in survival against the elements. It's only in most recent history that we've enjoyed the luxury to live, rather than simply survive. The fact is that the help and advice children need most nowadays has to do with a different level of survival in a world we've created ourselves, a complex world of rapid change.

Even though at moments nature can remind us of her often terrible wrath and power, most of our problems are still manmade. What we—parents and children both—have to learn is to deal with a reality that we have created ourselves.

In the bewildering array of cultures, creeds, and cross-purposes that are modern life, we need a special set of skills to live and be productive. Competition is an essential fact of life. Your child faces stress and pressure from society's expectations from the day he or she is born. To get through, your child needs the best help you can give.

The position of the professional expert is new and revered in our society. The expert is one of our cleverest inventions. Involved in the intense study of one problem or subject, the expert comes to know it better than anyone else. We trust the expert because we know that we don't have the time or ability to sort out everything ourselves. And, if the expert follows the best instincts of his profession, his high level of professional competence will serve you. By using the specialized knowledge of the expert, parents can face the difficult but practical problems of building a family and preparing their children to meet the demands of early childhood and elementary school.

Enlightened by this advice, we can give our children a healthy attitude and a better chance.

These concise and practical books deal with some of the most important issues in young children's lives today. They will help you to help your child and to feel good about your role as a parent. With this in mind, we dedicate this series to you.

Richard H. Thiel, Ph.D.
California State University

INTRODUCTION

D id you ever stop to think about how thrilled your parents were when you took your first step? Can you remember your father's joy and pride the first day you were able to pedal your two-wheeler without those ridiculous training wheels or his strong hands holding you up? Or your first Little League victory or first part in a school play?

Children grow up fast, and what a process it is. Today, however, it seems that many parents are overly eager for their children to mature. It's not likely that they think of it that way. But as parents joyously and conscientiously mark every milestone, they are often anticipating the next step in a predictable life plan, hardly pausing to celebrate the past for the future that lies ahead. Even as the child is born, there is the search for preschool, kindergarten, and elementary school. Before a child is even graduated from high school, he must be planning where to go to college and what to study.

Sometimes parents seem to have no choice but to force their children to hurry and grow up. Divorced parents, single parents, and families in which both parents work all make more demands on a child to "act his age" . . . or beyond. Children are expected to make easy transitions from one household to another, from relating to parent to teacher to after-care worker. A child is often expected to come home and amuse himself until a parent is there to take care of him.

Unfortunately, while we have yet to determine any real advantages to growing up too fast, there are many negative repercussions. The problem, however, is not necessarily a reflection on an individual parent or family; rather, it's a complex matter of parenting styles, social circumstances, and cultural expectations. This book is designed to help you understand how the subtle process of growing up can be thrown off balance by the pressure to grow up too quickly. The material contained here is divided into three parts. Part One is a brief overview of the phenomenon of growing up too fast and how trends in today's family life influence the problem. Part Two shows you how to take a closer look at your child. Part Three describes the strategies you can use to prevent your child from growing up too fast.

We hope the insights presented here will help you understand more about your child and how the pressures he may feel from you, or school, or society may be adversely affecting his life and what you can do about it together. As in all books in this series, references typically refer to a child as "he." Please remember that we are thinking of your daughter as well. Girls, like boys, are susceptible to the forces that urge them to think and act beyond their years. Childhood is a precious time, one of experimentation and discovery. Your job is to help your child maximize his capabilities and compensate for failings, so that he may look forward to a life that will be happy, fulfilling, and worthwhile. It hardly seems that parents could want any less for their children.

Part I
Why Children
Grow Up Too Fast

There is a greater push these days for children to act older than they actually are. Sometimes unwittingly, we expect a five-year-old to act like a seven-year-old, a nine-year-old to act like an eleven-year-old.

This is partly because we have learned a great deal about children's physical and intellectual capabilities in recent years. Physically, we have been seeing records made in swimming, track, skiing, climbing, all kinds of activities that seemed incomprehensible years ago. Likewise, we are learning more about the brain and our intellectual capabilities and have come to understand that children can not only engage in athletic training at a more intense level than perhaps we previously thought, but that they are capable of learning at a much earlier age than we thought.

This does not necessarily mean that they should always be pushed to do so, however. Our culture may be producing brighter, more athletic, and more aware children, but amid our enthusiasm for maximizing their capabilities, we must weigh the risks and benefits of encouraging our children to reach for their limits at too early an age. There are prices to pay for expecting children to act older than their years, including increased anxiety (in both children and parents), increased stress with which children have to cope, and a lowered sense of self-esteem or self-worth.

Pushing a child too quickly may communicate the message that his present rate of progress is somehow unsuitable. This will obviously have negative effects on the child's psyche and—if his parents *insist* on pushing him—on the parent-child relationship. This is extremely important because the family bond, which provides nurturing and stability, is crucial to any child's development.

Although life expectancy is greater now than it ever has been, and we have more time than ever before, parents sometimes insist on pushing children to the point where they frequently display adolescent behavior as early as age ten. Therapists are concerned that our society seems to be asking children to become small adults. Children today live in a culture where opportunities are considerably greater than what we experienced at their age. And although parents want the most for their children, some experts are beginning to suggest that our desire for our children's achievement may have less than selfless motivations. Some parents, for example, may expect their children to make up for their own lack of success, while others want their children to live up to their standards of success.

Unfortunately, the fact is that no matter how much a child might want to meet his parents' expectations, there *are* limits to his innate capabilities. Parents sometimes lose contact with the fact that normal childhood growth and development happens both forward and backward. In other words, they feel frustrated when their precocious five-year-old acts like he's three, while at other times he thrills them by acting with the poise of a child of seven. The problem is that they tend to reward the child when he pretends to be seven and reprimand him when he "acts his age." This can take the joy and fun out of childhood; it restrains children at exactly the time when they should be discovering their world, investigating, "acting silly," making mistakes, and discovering their own limits. Perhaps your child knows better than you can remember the spontaneity of childhood. And perhaps the five-year-old who suddenly disintegrates into the nonsensical behavior of someone less than his age is only trying to remind you of that.

Research seems to say that a child's own opinion of himself and his capabilities is more important than any other factor related to his overall mental health. Unfortunately, our society tends to reward children who are above average while neglecting those called average or "normal." We seem to have adopted exceptional intelligence and performance. This puts the child of average capabilities at an extreme disadvantage. Being average is no longer acceptable. *The exception has become the rule.*

There is an additional factor in our expectations

of our children: We live in a society with a very large middle class; one of the ways to gain distinction for ourselves and our offspring is to excel. Our society fosters competitiveness among children. Even without telling them directly, we let them know what is expected of them. And because children are very tuned in to their parents, they learn the messages early. Some families want so much to achieve that parents enroll in programs like the Baby Institute, where they learn to show flash cards to their young children, help them distinguish between types of classical music, and learn how to tell a Rembrandt from a Van Gogh.

Growing up too fast is new. We know for example, that average performance, or norms, on IQ tests are continually changing. You may remember taking the Stanford-Binet IQ test some thirty years ago and achieving a score of, say, 100. Since the same number of correctly answered questions on the Stanford-Binet today would indicate a score of 80. The questions asked on the test are based on the general pool of information thought to be available to children at any given time. The tests are routinely renormed, which means that the test "expects" more from students today because the general information pool is bigger, reflecting the amount of material children are exposed to. Concerned parents may compare their own IQ scores with those of their children and become alarmed. It's difficult to explain to them that their score of 145, achieved thirty years ago, is roughly comparable to their child's score of 120 today. "What's wrong?" they ask. "Nothing," is the answer.

Parents who may be concerned that their child

lacks in innate ability need to understand that intelligence involves many factors, including quickness of learning, the ability to learn general information, and to think in concepts. And all of these factors are related to a child's age and stage in life. For example, it is obvious that on virtually every task a nine-year-old child will be outperformed by a fifteen-year-old, whereas a five-year-old would not be able to match what a nine-year-old can do.

The raw measure of your child's intelligence may seem important to you because, in our competitive society, nobody wants a "dumb kid." Parents in many cases will experience a greater sense of value knowing that their child is "bright." For the most part, our intelligence is more closely related to our parents' intelligence than to our environment. This is true even in cases of children adopted from birth—their IQ values will be closer to those of their birth parents than their adoptive parents, regardless of the environment provided by the adoptive parents. So for many parents, their child's intelligence and capabilities may become important for their own ego and sense of self-esteem.

SOCIAL AND CULTURAL FACTORS AFFECTING ACHIEVEMENT

Given your child's natural ability, however, there are a number of factors that affect his intelligence and achievement. It's helpful to take a brief look at them here.

Nursery School

There is no doubt that more and more children

these days attend nursery school or preschool. For working parents, nursery school may have originally served the purpose of providing day-care for their children, but it gradually has become a permanent and influential fact of our children's lives. Far from providing simple childcare services, nursery school has become a source of early learning for children.

Learning that used to happen in kindergarten or first grade is now offered in nursery school. For example, it used to be that most children this age hadn't yet been to a store, so it fell to their teacher to take them. Before the visit, children would be prepared by naming the drawings or wooden replicas of fruits and vegetables in their classroom. This would be followed by an actual field trip. Once in the store, the children might pretend to shop by figuring the price of different items and instructions on how to buy various types of goods. Today, by the age of three, most children have probably shopped with their parents many times.

Parenting Classes

In the past parents did not seem to worry about how well they "did" at the job of raising their children. Recently, however, a new concept has developed and is receiving quite a following—"parenting." The idea that your actions can have an impact on a child and his sense of self-esteem is very new. Even the term *parenting* wasn't around a generation ago.

Previous parenting concepts were simple. If a child did something unpredictable or uncharacteristic, particularly something negative, the child was thought to be "bad," and the solution was to apply more discipline. Today most parents would scoff at that notion. Today it is a trend for parents to go to parenting classes and read parenting books for guidelines on how to raise their children. They attend "Mommy and Me" classes. We have PET (Parent Effectiveness Training) classes, stepparenting classes, and Confident Parenting classes. Courts are often recommending that divorcing parents enroll in these classes. Additionally, during the mediation process of divorce, parents are often taught parenting techniques and tools.

Classes for Children

Along with the parenting classes for adults, we are seeing the additional phenomenon of classes for children. There are exercise classes for infants and toddlers, and children can take classes in computer skills even at preschool age. What children learn in school is changing so that some advanced schools offer two years of kindergarten—after preschool.

Not all children adapt well or are prepared for this kind of experience. Take the case of Stacey, a four-and-a-half-year-old preschooler who couldn't write very well. Her teachers compared her to the other children in the class, who seemed able to write their letters, and became alarmed at her lack of progress. Stacey was very anxious and depressed—all unnecessary because her problem was simply that she did not yet have the fine motor skills needed for penmanship. Her progress had nothing to do with intelligence.

Stacey's case exemplifies the apprehension of a growing tide of parents who are concerned about what their children study in kindergarten and first grade, even though there's little data to support the idea that early learning (at ages four and five, for example) produce a generally more intelligent child. In fact, studies on early reading actually show that by the fourth grade the later readers have caught up with the early readers, and the two are almost the same.

Educational Choice

Due to the rising standard of living of the middle class, private schooling is now an option for many more children than it was years ago. And parents frequently expect much more from private schools than from public schools. Although they often express this as *more* or *different* learning, parents are not always sure just what that means; even worse, they may not know what is best for their child.

Unfortunately, private and parochial schools tend to add to parents' anxiety. Some parents who put their children into a special learning situation (which may also carry a hefty price tag)—expect their children to be spared the normal challenges and difficulties of growing up. A mother worried about her kindergartner reversing his letters, for example, is overly concerned. Reversing letters is normal for that age, and for some children, if not all, "extra" or more intense instruction will change this process.

Television

A characteristic of our society is the amount of television which children watch. Aside from some of the more distressing effects of early television watching, there is also the fact that some children's programs, such as "Sesame Street," have exposed children to learning opportunities they wouldn't have had before. These shows can have positive effects, but there is no doubt that the conventional media help pressure our children to grow up too quickly. The images of young children on TV are unrealistic. TV children don't yell and throw tantrums; they are charming and well behaved. If they have a problem, they are able to tell their parents about it very clearly. Most of all, TV children are encouraged to act far beyond their years.

Parents themselves are susceptible to the effects of TV and expect things from their own children based on what television shows. Unfortunately for parents and children, these images are often false. And unless they realize this is happening, parents can end up wanting one of these television children—one who causes few problems, is predictable, and meets or exceeds parental expectations. The combination of television-conditioned parent and television-conditioned child can create problems in family relationships.

The television problem isn't easy to solve; however, there are some precautions you can take, such as controlling not only the time your child spends in front of the set but what he watches. Additionally, the less time a child watches TV alone, the better. You can help minimize the unrealistic effects of television by talking with your children about events and characters as they appear on the screen. You can help your child understand the action and point out where the parents and child aren't realistic.

Television programs imply that all problems can be solved. Even children sense that this is not always true. When their parents are divorced and they want them back together, they know, no matter what, there isn't going to be a happy ending. Other problems may hit closer to home—a child who struggles with his friendships or can't control his anger. Although these problems *can* be solved, it is only with effort and time and energy, which is not the way television usually presents the situation or its outcome.

Cable television, especially, has provided exposure to movies children might not ordinarily see and which aren't suitable for them. Even cartoons have changed. Twenty years ago, for example, violence in a cartoon like "Road Runner" and "Bugs Bunny" took the form of a character being shoved off a cliff or running into a mountain. Today, because of technological advances, characters disintegrate with one zap of a ray gun or are easily shot down by computer-controlled spaceships. Aggression is much more hostile, and death, rather than temporary incapacitation or befuddlement, is the end result. (For a more complete discussion of children and television, see the companion book *How to Be a Good Role Model for Your Child*.)

"Let's Be Honest"

Many experts feel that the pendulum has swung a little too far in being honest and open with children. There is no doubt that sometimes it can go overboard—in divorce cases, for example, where parents believe they should be totally honest with their children. It's impossible for a child to deal well with his mother telling him "honestly" that "the reason Daddy left is because he has a girlfriend," or complaining to the child that he can't have the latest *Star Wars* laser gun because "Dad's not paying child support anymore." Nor can a child help but feel threatened when he is asked, "Do you know that Mom's drinking a lot?" Although a parent may say such things with the best of intentions, that kind of honesty can actually be hostile.

Take Paul, for example, a ten-year-old whose parents recently divorced. He spends weekends with his father, and the rest of the week he lives with his mother. Because his parents are in the midst of a difficult and angry divorce, Paul's life has changed. He is now being asked to deal with the situation by being more "grown-up." With his father no longer living in the home and his mother working full-time, Paul is required to be responsible for things that were previously taken care of for him. For example, he now has to make his own bed in the morning and prepare his own lunch. And he is being forced to listen to his mother's frustrations. To show how parents can fall into this trap with their children, let's listen in on a conversation between Paul and his mother:

Mom: *I know it's more difficult around here now. You just need to do more because your father is not contributing the child support like he was supposed to do.*

Paul: *What do you mean, Mom?*

Mom: *Dad was supposed to contribute money each month, but he's not doing it now, so we don't have any extra spending money. In fact, the reason I have to work so hard is because he doesn't contribute to the family.*

Paul: *Gee, Mom, I thought Dad was giving us money. He told me he was.*

Mom: *He was supposed to give us more. He lives in a nice place, but he doesn't want to give us any more money, and we can't get along. In fact, he took a lot of the furniture that wasn't even his. My mother gave me some of the furniture, and he just took it.*

Paul: *Are you sure he would do something like that?*

Mom: *Yes, and I'll tell you something else. He doesn't want to pay for your special school next year. He doesn't even care about that. So you may have to go to public school next semester.*

What parents like Paul's mother fail to realize is that divorce is an adult problem, and children shouldn't have to take sides. Paul was very upset and felt very much like a ball being tossed between both parents. Trying to deal with a threatening and anxiety-producing situation, Paul withdrew. He stopped doing his homework, he stopped playing with his friends, and he stopped talking with his parents about anything he felt might be controversial. As things continued to get worse, Paul's teacher reported that he was fighting with the other children and not paying attention in class.

There is no doubt there are things that happen to parents and other adults that young children just shouldn't know. Often it is a child's behavior itself that evokes a parent's statement of honesty, especially when parents "share" their emotions—perhaps one or another's reaction to how a child has upset him. Although this may be an honest response to what the child did, it is *not* a healthy thing to do.

Therapists are shocked to know very young children who can tell them how much they have in their bank account—or worse, their parents' bank account—or how much their parents paid for their cars, or even their father's salary. If a child of five, six, or seven can't understand the content or significance of such information, there is no reason for him to be receiving it. Therapists fear that parents' motivation may be desire to seem more important in the child's eyes.

Details about divorce, difficulties between parents, and financial problems shouldn't be shared with children. A child wants to like both his parents, and when they give him inappropriate information, they're asking him to take sides. Additionally, as in Paul's mother's case, a parent may also inadvertently be asking the child to participate in his or her problems.

Values and Modeling

Parents are often far too casual when talking with

children about their values and the role models they have chosen for themselves. Although it may be OK for a parent to admire someone whom he thinks is successful because that person has earned a great deal of money, this is a very limited a definition of success. What about the librarian down the street who has devoted her life to teaching minority children to read, or even the child's own teacher? Too often, being successful means being the best; even then, "the best" is typically defined in terms of money and material wealth.

Children easily absorb their parents' interests in material success. Therapists regularly see young children worried about the labels on their clothes—children who want Reebok shoes or Jordache jeans or Guess outfits. These are not things that a young child should be thinking about. Children do not come to value things such as the make of clothing by themselves. Although there may be peer pressure involved, these types of values are also taught in the home.

Parents often commit this error unintentionally by talking in front of a child about their own concerns without understanding they are actually teaching their child values by doing so. Even if parents themselves are interested in designer jeans, they should keep quiet in front of their children. All parents should always be aware, however, that children can easily tell the difference between what you say and what you do. Raising a child and teaching him the right values for a happy and healthy life—and giving that child time to grow up and develop his values—is the most important job a parent has.

THE CHANGING FAMILY

Aside from changes in what we expect from our children, differences in the family also affect the child who is forced—or chooses—to grow up too fast.

Single Parents

Forty-five percent of all children will have experienced living with just one parent by the time they're eighteen. This is a far cry from thirty years ago, when it was unusual to hear of single-parent families. Being from a single-parent home may put pressure on a child to grow up early. In most cases, the single parent must work, forcing the younger child into some kind of day-care.

Because such a child spends more time outside the home, there will be pressure on him to be well behaved. Also, the normal child toilet-trains at about two and a half to three years old; the process is often hastened, however, because most day-care centers require a child to be toilet-trained. Thus parents, pressured by such requirements, will often expect a younger child to show a level of self-restraint and cooperation that is really the kind of behavior appropriate to older children.

Furthermore, because of the increase in single-parent homes and in two-working-parent homes, children are asked to do more on their own. Although it makes it easier on the parents if their children can help out, it becomes a problem when parents expect them to do more than they can do. We know that a child needs help and guidance. He needs a parent to sit down with him at times to check his progress and direct him. Expecting a child to do too many things on his own just isn't healthy. The ten-year-old latchkey child who is expected to come home by himself, do his homework, get a snack, and set the table for dinner is a child who is expected to do more than he's capable of doing. And, unfortunately, it's not that uncommon.

Because children are children, they want to do what their parents want, especially when there is little parent-child interaction, and rules are strict and unbendable. Too much of this, however, is not healthy. The overly compliant child often doesn't move away from his parents; he is often late in developing personal independence or may fail to do so altogether. Sometimes these children are afraid to make their opinions known and are fearful in unfamiliar situations. Often they are so pressured that they're afraid to say no to something a parent wants.

Parenting is the most difficult job in the world even when there are two of you, so being a single parent is an extremely difficult task. There's a lot of pressure to fulfill both parents' roles. For the single mom, this may mean taking the son to the ball field at the same time she worries about her daughter's need for ballet lessons.

Effects of Divorce

A child of a divorce must often adjust to two environments; he may live with one parent and visit the other, or custody may be shared. This situation requires complex emotional adjustments by children

at any age. Young children particularly are not prepared to deal with the breakup of their home. Unfortunately, parents, suffering their own emotional tur-
moil, may expect their children to behave like a
trooper and to take care of themselves as they are
shuffled from one to another. In this situation, parents often complain that during the first few hours
after the child comes home from the other parent's
house, he is extremely difficult to control. The child
may also tell each parent that he doesn't want to go
to the other's house, reflecting an unconscious wish
that the parents remain together.

Often the rules are different in each household.
Sometimes children are inadvertently encouraged
by one parent to misbehave in the other's house.
One parent—trying to impress the other with his or
her parenting—encourages the child to be well behaved and perhaps act older when he visits the other
parent.

A child can have one overindulgent parent and one
underindulgent parent. A child may spend most of
the time with his father watching TV, for example,
but when he's with his mother (who feels that the
child's experiences with the father are poor), every
moment is planned. The danger in underindulgence
is neglect; overindulgence often causes the child to
fail to develop skills he will need to cope with life.

Effects of Two Working Parents

One of the biggest changes in the family over the last
twenty years is the number of households in which
both parents work. This tremendous change has ma-

jor effects on parenting and growing up too fast. First, there are the problems with day-care. Additionally, the child may have to deal with after-school care; he is expected to get himself to the aftercare, do his homework, and pack his book bag before he plays with other children. Certainly, that's something you can ask a twelve-year-old to do—but not even all twelve-year-olds are capable of it. Even after the child gets home, he's expected to take his bath and get into pajamas while his parents make dinner.

Parents often say, "Well, he did it last week," or, "He did it beautifully on Monday." However, the fact that a child can do something on Monday and Tuesday doesn't mean he can do it Wednesday and Thursday. Under ideal circumstances, a child may be able to perform, but he is often unable to adapt if something goes wrong. If you threaten and lambaste a child enough, he will respond; this doesn't mean that he can do the job all the time. It doesn't mean that without that kind of threat, the child can do it on his own. Such children might grow up obedient, but they also grow up unhappy.

In fact compliance is *not* the mark of a healthy child. *Healthy children sometimes say no.* If you expect your child to go along with everything you want him to do, you're squashing his growth. Parents complain that they shouldn't need to remind their child to brush his teeth. But the fact is, many parents don't really know about what their child can do. Six-year-olds don't even *want* to brush their teeth; they do it because mom and dad tell them to do it. It's a learned habit. That means, whether you like it or not, as parents you will need to do a lot of reminding until your child has really learned what's required of him. This does not mean that you should nag or be critical, but that you should continually enforce a routine until the child has learned it. Even then, expect that your child will not always do what you want him to do, and that he will fall back occasionally. Such challenges are often much more acute in families where both parents work.

Decline of the Extended Family

The extended family has all but disappeared in this country. Families are scattered, and older family members, such as grandparents, spend more time in the job market than previously. This means they aren't as available for childcare as they were in the past. This contributes to the difficulties faced by single parents and families with two working parents. There is no way out of the fact that their children will be spending large amounts of time in group situations supervised by adults who have little emotional ties to them.

In a single-parent home or one with two working parents, children often have very little to say about what's happening to them. They go to school, to aftercare, and to the sitter. Previously, much of this time would have been occupied by a visit to a grandmother or to an aunt or uncle. A child shuttled back and forth from one impersonal situation to another will eventually begin to feel powerless. Children need to feel they have some say in what's happening in their lives. This can be remedied partially during the time spent in the family, especially quality play time, when the child can feel that it's OK to interact and tell his parents what's going on and how he feels about his life.

THE CRITICAL IMPORTANCE OF SELF-ESTEEM

Simply stated, self-esteem is the feeling we have about ourselves and our capabilities. Self-esteem is rarely neutral. We usually speak of lowered self-esteem when a person feels bad about himself. On the other hand, when a person feels good about himself and is moving ahead full bore, we say he has a healthy sense of self-esteem. This means the person has a high level of self-regard; he honors and respects himself for the person he is and has admiration and regard for his capabilities.

Children who have a high level of self-esteem have low levels of anxiety. They feel good about themselves; they're likely to have higher academic and social success. A child with high self-esteem feels he can conquer problems. The unfortunate child with a low sense of self-esteem is anxious. He often feels overwhelmed, dazed, confused, and unprepared. When a problem arises, he feels too weak to get himself out of his difficulties.

A solid sense of self-esteem doesn't just happen. It's developed—primarily through the opportunities a child has to test himself. If a parent constantly protects a child, does things for him, shelters him from life's demands, plies him with gifts that distract him but do nothing to help him develop his own imagination, the parent is effectively guaranteeing the child will not feel good about himself. Unless a child is allowed to try, to fail, and to learn from his failures (which means that he is not unduly criticized for mistakes), he will never know what he can do and what he can't. He will never have the thrill of attempting a difficult task and accomplishing it; he will never learn his limits.

A healthy sense of self-esteem is crucial for good growth. Too often, a child who is rushed through his early years will find himself in trouble. Some children of whom too much is expected will just give up. Others will constantly struggle, trying to do too much without a moment to stop to see what they've done.

Sometimes parents will actually do their child's schoolwork. The child will then be faced with having to perform beyond his abilities when called on in class, and very often he will fail. A child in this situation feels constantly off-guard and is doomed to have a very weak sense of himself, which in turns translates into an extremely lowered sense of self-esteem. In striving to keep their child from failing, such parents practically guarantee that he will.

For children, especially, self-esteem often is a kind of "inner speech." Children learn the material of this inner speech from parents and other authority figures. If you say to a child, for example, "You know, Samantha, that's a terrific thing you're drawing. Your colors are beautiful, your strokes are clean, you're really doing a *very* nice job," you are not only encouraging the child at the moment you're speaking to her, but you are providing a model of how she can talk to herself when she's in a similar situation. If instead you say, "You know what . . . I can tell that's a tree, but *you* know that trees are brown, they're not blue. Why did you draw a blue tree?" you would be destroying the child's sense of accomplishment. You are also modeling inner dialogue she will later use to withdraw when she's asked to do something creative.

When a parent constantly corrects a child, the child takes to heart what the parent says. And with that message going around and around in his head, the child will never learn to feel OK about himself or what he does. His self-esteem will always be on shaky ground. In trying to meet his parents' expectations, (which he senses have little to do with his ability), he will become overly stressed and unable to develop.

THE OVERINDULGED CHILD

More and more therapists are noticing a persistent pattern among children who are rushed through childhood. We call it "the overindulged child." This child's problems are often the result of parents' good intentions to "give their child everything." Unfortunately, the overindulged child is in danger of not being able to grow up. He will end up short on imagination, needing to be stimulated, and burned out before he reaches his teens. In his teens, the overindulged child is in the greatest danger of getting into trouble with sex, alcohol, or drugs. Overindulgence is not necessarily the result of a child having too much. Sometimes he doesn't have enough.

Generally, the overindulged child is overburdened

with a surplus of riches, so to speak. Such a child is easily identified by the following traits:

● *His clothes*—A young child for whom it is very important to wear very expensive brand-name clothing is overindulged.

● *His time*—The overindulged child never has a spare moment; his day is planned for him, and he is expected to go through his paces. He is enrolled in dance, karate, or computer class, or is on a sports team. He has a tutor if his grades slip. His parents encourage an active social life. The indulged child lacks an important part of childhood: the time to just *be*.

● *His enthusiasm*—The overindulged child is bored easily. He must be constantly busy; he must have the latest toys and follow the latest craze. No place, activity, or object is special for the overindulged child. It's *essential* that your child develop his own set of needs and desires. It's motivating for a child to be able to select what he wants to do with his time, and he not be forced to proceed through an endless round of what his parents want him to do. This provides crucial protection against your child giving up and withdrawing—what therapists often refer to as "childhood burnout."

● *His capacity to want*—An indulged child often has everything, sometimes before he even knows he wants it. In many cases, in fact, it is not he who wants it, but his parents—and not always for the right reasons. Take Jonathan, for example. Jonathan is smart. He is also from a very wealthy family and is aware of their wealth. Recently he told his mother

how much he liked the aquarium in his pediatrician's waiting room. A week later, Jonathan had his
own fully stocked aquarium. Not only that, but because his mother was concerned Jonathan wouldn't
take proper care of the fish (and since she didn't
care to do so herself), she arranged for a service
company to come twice a month to clean the aquarium and check the plants and fish. By providing the
service contract, Jonathan's parents deprived him
of the experience of taking responsibility for the
aquarium and understanding the consequences of
having a pet. They also deprived themselves of an
opportunity to share time with their son. Making the
care of the aquarium a family project would have
been beneficial to Jonathan and would have added a
dimension to his relationship with his parents.

Jonathan's experience is not uncommon. More and
more homes have regular help—maids and house-
keepers—as well as gardeners and pool cleaners . . .
and aquarium services. A child in such an environment often has no sense of doing for himself. He
doesn't even know what it means to pick up his
clothes or make his bed. What he knows about clean
clothes may involve little more than the fact that if
he drops his clothes on the floor one day, they will
reappear in his drawers a few days later, clean and
ready to wear.

   ● *His attention span*—An overindulged child
has difficulty keeping himself interested in projects
or activities. He quickly loses his passion for a project. Unfortunately, his parents don't require him to
face his boredom. Either they aren't disciplined
enough to force the child to complete what he's

started, or they take his random interest in things as above-average intelligence and encourage him to roam through a variety of uncompleted experiences. Because of this, an overindulged child constantly looks for beginnings.

• *His lack of persistence*—Overindulged children are easily frustrated because they are used to having their parents solve their problems for them. At the same time, they set very high standards for themselves. This is a losing proposition on all counts, because if a child's parent does the work for him, the child is robbed of the experience of trying and succeeding or failing and then trying again. Additionally, since the parent is the one who is completing the work and is obviously better at it than the child, the child is in danger of expecting that he should do as well as his parents. He will not complete a drawing or a painting because he can't do it like he thinks he wants to.

Betsy is an excellent example of a child who will not attempt anything that she doesn't already know she's the best at. If she has an assignment to draw something, she'll go in her room, lock her door, and work at the drawing until she feels it's perfect. If she can't do it the way she wants to, she becomes angry and destroys her work. Betsy's problem is that she's not comfortable with herself and feels her work should be as good as older children's. There is no doubt that for healthy development, a child has to learn to be comfortable with being a child. If he doesn't learn this at an early age, he will have more significant difficulties in his teens because awkwardness is a way of life for children. One of the reasons children want to act older or hang around with older children is to reduce this sense of awkwardness. Our society reinforces that desire, complimenting children for looking older than they are or acting more sophisticated than their age.

● *His understanding of cause and effect—* Another sign of overindulgence is the child who has never learned the consequences of his actions. Often parents add to the problem. Rachel's mother, for example, simply won't allow her child to fail a spelling test. There are two spelling tests each week in Rachel's advanced class. The first test is returned so the children can prepare for the second. By agreement with her mother, Rachel is supposed to look up the words she missed and their definitions and write them out as a way of solidifying the spelling and concept of the word. One night Rachel refused to do the work required to prepare for the second test. She complained of a headache and said she preferred to watch TV. Horrified that she might fail the test, Rachel's mother set to work on the assignment and then sat with Rachel until she had carefully copied the words and definitions her mother had looked up. Another classic example of parental interference in the cause-and-effect chain is the science project where the child actually gets in the way of his *parents'* efforts to do an excellent project.

There's a message here from parent to child, and it says, "You cannot do this project as well as I can, and it's very important to me that you get a good mark. Therefore, I don't want you to try; I'll do it." The parent's need for the child to excel, however, detracts from the child's feeling of worth, especially if the parent will not allow him the opportunity to try and fail. The child begins to feel that he's unable to do anything without the parent's active involvement because he is not good enough. This destructive message from parent to child says, "You—nine-year-old Jimmie—cannot do this as well as I—thirty-five-year-old Daddy. When you're older, you will probably do it better." The child may hear this as, "Hurry up and grow up so you can please me with what you do."

A child who grows up with this kind of pressure from his parents will have a constant need to look to an authority figure for approval. He will not be able to depend on his own sense of accomplishment. He will instead depend on his parents or teachers to say his work is OK. What a frightful way to go through life.

THE UNDERINDULGED CHILD

Interestingly enough, the overindulged child often shows signs of the other common syndrome among children, the underindulged child. The underindulged child is not simply an economically disadvantaged child. Many an underindulged child is found in affluent households. An underindulged child's problem is he receives *insufficient* attention from his parents. The parents may be absent a lot, either because they work or are preoccupied with their own activities. Even if the parents are physically present, they may be unwilling or unable to spend quality time with their children. They may provide presents, toys, elaborate playtime activities—but it is a nanny, teacher, or governess who plays with and cares for the child, not the parents.

Predictably, an underindulged child has few intellectual experiences. His parents don't actively expose him to such things; they might not even watch a quality television show with their child or read a book to him. They seldom talk about the value of education. Or they may so overwhelm the child with the need to succeed in school that the child becomes obsessed with his academic progress. This is not nurturing, however; this is task mastering—and a sign of underindulgence on the parents' part. They may provide the goals but not help and aid. Their child then becomes a mini-adult struggling with his difficulties on his own.

The underindulged child has few family experiences. The family doesn't go on outings, play sports, or do household chores together. Such parents don't think of a simple thing like taking a walk together or taking time to discuss things with their children. As a result, the child will distrust people and be afraid to depend on them.

While you're teaching your child independence, you also have to teach him dependence. A young child needs to know that it's OK to depend on Mom and Dad, that his family represents security, and that he's not hanging out there all alone. This means, of course, that Mom and Dad have to be available. You have to provide your child with certain experiences and keep him safe. The underindulged child is always rushing one step ahead of his anxieties.

As parents, we owe some responsibility to our children to be there for them. A housekeeper or nanny cannot replace Mom or Dad. A preschool teacher or day-care worker cannot provide the same quality of love and care. It's fine to have help in the house as long as you also spend time with your children and don't give care-taking responsibilities entirely to the hired help.

Generally, parents of an underindulged child have little interest in his school homework, extracurricular activities, or social life. As a result, the child may feel unwanted and look to other sources of belonging—his peers, for example. (This kind of child has been found to be extremely susceptible to peer pressure.) Unfortunately this is often a matter of parents' priorities. For example, parents who both have jobs may not have time to look at a child's homework, go to a school open house, talk to the scoutmaster, attend a ball game, or share activities. Often there's little if any parent-child interaction.

Rob's parents, for example, are both extremely bright and hold doctoral degrees—she in mathematics, he in physics. Rob's father drops him off at childcare at 7:30 A.M., and his mother picks him up between 6:00 and 6:30 P.M. Rob's bedtime is 7:30, which doesn't leave much time for his parents to spend with him. Rob, who is four, is already showing signs of "old age." He's not interested in the children his age at nursery school; he prefers to play with the first-grader down the street. Rob doesn't behave well in preschool and is a constant source of irritation to his teachers because he's always questioning what they ask him to do. He has no chores to do at home because the family has a full-time maid. To amuse himself Rob has taken to experimenting with different chemicals and cleaners in the house. One day he made a cake with shoe polish and grass and flavored it with brown sugar. When the maid wasn't looking, he put the "cake" in the oven, turned on the gas, and within ten minutes the whole thing exploded, damaging the stove and part of the kitchen cabinets.

Rob was referred to therapy by the head of his preschool, who was threatening to expel him. He was so aggressive toward the other children that the staff couldn't leave him alone on the playground because he bit and pushed his classmates. He also took on the role of "protector" of younger children. For example, if a boy was chasing girls in his class, Rob made it his responsibility to stop him, even though this angered the other boy. What Rob was doing was providing protection for others that he didn't have in his own life. Rob was also a very cold child. Most children are affectionate, but Rob would not hug his teacher or any of the other day-care staff, or allow them to touch him in any way. His teacher admitted in her referral letter that she didn't like Rob very much and found little charm in him.

So, while Rob is probably one of the brightest children in his group, he doesn't know how to have relationships because he has so little interaction with the most important people in his life—his parents. He is basically growing up on his own, without benefit or guidance from his parents; because he has developed such a hostile personality, he receives little warmth from his teachers or friendship from his peers.

You should strive to have a happy, well-balanced

child who's able to perform well in various situations, who can socialize well with his peers, and who is able to concentrate on his schoolwork and complete tasks appropriate to his age and capabilities. Above all, it's important that your child should not be afraid of attempting new things.

The following part will help you identify the signs of a child who is growing up too fast so that you can slow down the process. If you don't, you may face even graver problems later in life, especially in adolescence. Statistics about teenage behavior are indeed troubling:

- Six thousand teens committed suicide during 1986; another five hundred thousand attempted it. One-third of all children who committed suicide did so after a failed love affair.
- Seventy percent of teenage girls who run away from home do so because they think they're pregnant. They may have engaged in early sex because they needed affection or because they wanted to appear older.
- Eleven percent of seventh- to tenth-graders can be classified as problem drinkers; children as young as nine have been reported to have drinking problems.
- Fifteen percent of all teens are considered vulnerable teenagers—those who will require therapy and other types of mental health intervention later in life.

All of these children are susceptible to behavior that doesn't fit their age and development and can be destructive. Most therapists would agree that many children who have a troubled adolescence are victims of being rushed through childhood. They constantly seek outlandish experiences or easy answers to the complicated problems of their lives. The good news is your child doesn't have to end up that way. *You* can help rescue your child from such a fate.

Part II
Taking A Look
at Your Child

Your expectations of your children are crucial to their healthy growth and development. Parents sometimes unconsciously convey to their children much higher expectations for behavior than they may be capable of. Sometimes this is directly related to the parents. They may want their children to live up to their own level of success or make up for the success they never had as a child. Sometimes parents unwittingly respond to the demands of society or their own peer groups. Other parents may unconsciously desire to parade their children's accomplishments as an extension of their own success. None of these circumstances is good for a child.

On the other hand, as we have seen, social changes have resulted in higher expectations for children to grow and mature at a more rapid rate. Sometimes it seems that there is no alternative. Single-parent families, divorced families, and families where both parents work are high-demand families. Everyone is stressed to the maximum. Parents caught between work, child rearing, and whatever social life they can grab for themselves frequently lose sight of the fact that their children are children and not adults. They expect too much of them. They are not with them enough to observe signs of problems or to nurture them with the special brand of loving care that only a parent can give. It is an overstatement, probably, to say that these children are neglected. Obviously, their parents are doing what they can to make the best possible life for their family, but often there is little they feel they *can* do.

Some children can handle themselves in this kind of situation; others can't. The sensitive child is particularly susceptible to anxiety and frustration from being pushed too fast too soon. In the following material we present a brief description of behavior that may indicate that your child is a victim of unwarranted expectations and overly rapid growth, which can lead to a critical loss of self-esteem. If you spot your child among these, keep reading. Part Three will tell you what to do.

It's important for you to observe your child in a detached manner. Clear away your emotions. You must learn what his strengths and weaknesses are. Does your child have musical ability? Does he make friends easily? Is he showing ability in one area of school but not another? You will need to observe your child so you can encourage him in those areas where he shows interest and feels competent and help him make up for where he may be weak.

It's important to get an idea of what's normal behavior for your child's age group. You can do this by informally observing your child with other children. Does he tend to stand out in some way? Is he less friendly, more aggressive, easier to calm down? In general, we expect young children to have friends, and you will want to assess your child's capability in this area, which is a crucial part of his childhood development. Is he invited places with other children? Does he talk enthusiastically of his friends?

Be as objective as possible when you observe your child. Wise parents will expect their children to be average in some areas, below average in others, and possibly excellent in still others. It's important that you come to terms with your child's weak points, so that you can say to yourself and others, "My child has a lot of problems with math, but he can tell you all the batting averages of all the major-league baseball players," or, "My daughter is a math whiz, but her handwriting's so bad I can't read it," or even better, "My child gets *B*s and *C*s in school, but he has a lot of interests and a lot of friends; I think he's happy and content."

Your observations should also include occasional input from your child's teachers, parents of his friends, and other adults who have frequently had contact with your child. Your goal in questioning teachers, coaches, scoutmasters, and other parents is simple: to further understand what is expected behavior, given your child's age and stage of development. You should ask whether any of these other adults have observed signs of strange actions in your child or perhaps can confirm difficulties you yourself have uncovered. The following section will guide you in your observations.

SIGNS OF A CHILD WHO IS GROWING UP TOO FAST

In assessing your child for signs that he is being pushed beyond his years, you should think in terms of degree. Outlandish displays of behaviors described below indicate you should seek professional help for your child. In the majority of cases, however, a simple adjustment of your attitude, especially your expectations, may well solve the problem and help you establish new patterns in your family. The following are the primary signs a child is growing up too fast:

1. He will want to be seen as being older than he really is. Most children seem to want to be older for a variety of reasons; they are impatient with restrictions their parents inflict on them and want more freedom to try their wings. Perhaps it is simply that a child doesn't have any friends his own age to play with; just as likely, however, he may be bored with his peers and so spends time by himself. Unfortunately, this is not entirely healthy behavior. For example, Ryan, a ten-year-old from a wealthy family, has a "hobby" of fixing cars. Glad that he had an interest and oblivious that it was not good for the boy to spend so much time by himself, Ryan's parents gave him his own car to tinker with. His mother reports that Ryan spends "every spare minute of his time" with his car, taking apart the engine, cleaning the parts, putting them back together. Ryan, how-ever, has few friends and while his classmates think he's a "nerd," he thinks they do silly or childish things and doesn't want to associate with them. He does well in school, especially in math and science, and his teachers have no complaints about his behav-ior. He tends to be quiet, and to stay by himself. Because he has isolated himself socially, Ryan's emo-tions seem more appropriate for a much younger child. He pulls silly pranks on his classmates, and he seems to enjoy being the class clown. Since he usu-ally completes assignments faster than other stu-dents, he is frequently bored in class and uses the time to think up his pranks. Ryan is an extreme ex-ample of a child who wants to act older because he doesn't relate to his peers, but many children who are pushed too hard will isolate themselves from their social group and attempt to identify with older children.

2. *He will be sexually interested beyond his age.* You should be on the lookout for the eleven- or twelve-year-old who shows an interest in sex that is more on the level of what would be expected of a teenager. Adolescents' sexual curiosity is part of the process of growing up, both physically and emotion-ally. This is not part of development in early child-hood, however. A thirteen-year-old who regularly has intercourse is acting beyond his years and his capacity to deal with the consequences of his behav-ior. Sidney, for example, is required to be home only one day of the weekend, and his family frequently has no idea where he is. Sidney's allowance, which is disproportionate to his age, allows him considerable

freedom to be away from home and to attract the kind of young girls who are also prematurely interested in sexual experimentation. Sidney receives $25 a week for "expenses," which include two movies a week, gas money for his older friends who provide transportation, restaurant meals, and extra clothes. Unfortunately, Sidney's behavior is not unusual; he is simply mirroring the standards mandated by the other members of his peer group. Sidney's early sexual exploration has other effects. First, it exposes him to children who are older than he and who may not necessarily provide the correct role models. Additionally, it puts him in a peer group that suffers from problems similar to his. His friends are overindulged in material things but lack care and nurturing. Sidney's parents are divorced; his stepfather, a judge, has helped Sidney's brother, who has been in trouble with numerous traffic violations and credit problems. When asked what would happen if he were to get into trouble, Sidney simply answers, "The judge will take care of it."

3. He is reluctant to try new things because of discomfort with his awkwardness. Such a child might not try to ride a bike because he fears he won't be able to do it as well as older children who are more coordinated. He might refuse to try to draw in class because he is afraid his work isn't as good as the other children's or the things his parents have done for him. This child isn't comfortable with himself and his capabilities . . . and he is very susceptible to burnout. He may be in the most advanced classes at school (this is often private school) and have won a number of honors for his accomplishments. Inside, however, he feels bad about himself.

4. He will become ill every time there's a Little League game or a test at school or when faced with any kind of stressful situation. This is a child under pressure. A child who cries a lot when he approaches his homework or anything where a certain level of performance is expected is being pushed too fast, either by his own or others' expectations. Not long ago, a pediatrician in an affluent California suburb took inventory and determined that his practice was filled with a group of routine patients who suffered from a variety of illnesses. If he solved the problem, the child would be back again with another. Chronic earaches turned into nausea, headaches into stomachaches. It was only after he insisted on referring chronic patients to a health facilitator who helped them sort out the things that were bothering them, in school or with their family, or friends that such children become well.

Children are acutely sensitive to stress in their environment. You should take any kind of chronic illness or complaint seriously as a sign your child may be disturbed emotionally. If parental efforts to determine the nature of the problem fail, then professional help is advised.

5. He suffers from a lowered sense of self-esteem. It is crucial for a child to develop an adequate sense of himself and his capabilities. Children who suffer from inadequate self-esteem frequently are pushed too hard. A parent who demands more of a child than the child can give physically, emotionally, or socially cannot escape the fact that the child will feel defeated. An inadequate sense of self-esteem shows up in a variety of ways. You should observe your child very carefully for these signs:

● Your child may talk negatively about himself. He may say to you, "I'm no good. I wish I wasn't born. I can't do anything right."

● He may demonstrate a consistently high level of anxiety, exhibited as chronic illness, or inappropriate behavior, such as crying and tantrums. Or he may be depressed. Worse, he will complain that he can't do anything about these difficulties.

● Unable to solve an emotional problem, he may attempt to disguise it in inappropriate behavior or as a physical ailment. Ronnie, for example, is in therapy. His parents, who are divorced, still have not resolved their difficulties and fight constantly. Ronnie identifies with his mother, which makes it difficult for him to leave her to visit his father. To forestall his visits to his father, Ronnie has developed a whole list of ailments—headaches, nausea, and stomachaches—that prevent him from keeping his obligation to his father. The problem is compounded by the fact that Ronnie misses a lot of school because of his illnesses.

● He may have problems sleeping or have nightmares. Before you jump to conclusions, check to see if he is watching too much TV. One child whose nightmares were so bad that he was referred to a therapist had his own TV in his room, with access via cable to adult-rated films.

● He may spend time playing alone and have few or no friends.

● He may talk about feeling depressed. A child may not know the word, of course, but if he sleeps a lot, lacks cheer, and seems generally defeated for more than two weeks at a time, you should explore the possibility that he is suffering from depression.

 ● He may show a strong desire for perfection in everything he does. A child who always needs to get As, always needs to hit the bull's-eye, is really saying he's worthy of your attention only when he is at peak performance.

These cues to a rushed child are only so many words on paper if you do not spend time with your child and assess his behavior. This doesn't necessarily mean you should make a big deal of the observation process but that it should be part of the daily life you live with your children.

THE IMPORTANCE OF PEER RATINGS

In one interesting project, researchers attempted to determine whether it would be possible to forecast at the third-grade level which children would require therapy or treatment with mental health professionals or referral for counseling in their teen years. The researchers asked parents to rate their child according to such questions as, "Do you like your child?" They also asked teachers to rate the children and had children rate each other. The researchers evaluated attendance records, health records, and intelligence factors. They attempted to assess any variables that might show a child was "at risk," meaning he would later seek or be referred for mental health counseling.

After evaluating all their data, the researchers found that the greatest single predictor of overall mental health was what they called peer ratings—

how a child stood with his peers. It didn't matter how the teachers evaluated a child or how bright he was; what did matter was whether the child was liked and accepted by his peers. Did other children want to spend time with him? Did they consider him a good friend? Was he well liked? Therapists report that often their first question of a child is about his standing with his peers. "Tell me about your friends," they will ask the child. "Do you have friends? What's your reputation at school?" Parents concerned about their child's development should ask the same questions instead of concentrating on other factors—intelligence, academics, or athletic skills—especially if they are obsessed with their child being the best, the first, the finest. Instead of awards and medals, they should be wondering whether their child is a good friend.

Most report cards report progress in academic subjects, work habits, and cooperation. But nowhere is there a grade for being a good friend, for being well liked, for being considerate or kind. Yet these are values that will prove to be more important than whether or not your child can print neatly.

Researchers have described several factors that contribute to a child's being well liked:

- The child comes from a home where parents like their children.
- His parents give him a lot of praise.
- Discipline is never demeaning or shameful to the child. His parents are smart enough to call him away from the group when they need to chastise him; they don't spank the child in front of others;

they employ more nonviolent types of discipline such as sending the child to his room or discussing with him why his behavior is inappropriate.

• The rules in the home are clear, fair, and restrictive. This child knows his limits; he's not over-indulged, nor is he neglected. Setting clear limits lowers anxiety in children. The companion book *Creating a Good Self-Image in Your Child* is a helpful source for information on how to manage effective family communication and rule-setting.

A child who is raised with this quality of life tends to be kind to other children. He knows how to go up to another child and ask, "Are you OK? Do you want to play with my ball?" He is also more empathic and tends to be able to identify feelings in himself and in others (a sign of good self-esteem). Such a child doesn't have to make another feel bad to make himself feel good. He can feel good about himself when someone else succeeds. Like adults, a child can only give when he feels "full." If he feels empty emotionally, he won't give to someone else, and he'll feel as if something is being taken away if giving becomes required. The "full" child, the one who feels best about himself, can give to someone else, can help someone else, can be a friend to someone else. It's a sign of high self-esteem and lowered anxiety, and it's a value that will serve a child throughout his life.

THE STAGES OF DEVELOPMENT

A tremendous amount of brain development takes place during childhood (ages five through twelve).

This is when children learn to write, to copy, and to understand cause and effect. A significant amount of development also occurs in the areas of logical analysis, concept formation, and abstract reasoning.

Erik Erikson refers to this as the age of Industry versus Inferiority and maintains that reasoning begins to develop during this stage. Jean Piaget calls it the age of "Concrete Operation," when the child learns to manipulate objects, deal with classifications, and assemble like items in a series. Logical thought begins to occur. The child's brain has begun to develop as a central processing computer.

By the age of nine, the type of thinking required of children changes. Parents and teachers ask them processing types of questions, such as "What do you think about this? What's the main idea of the story you just read?" Such questions require asking children to use logical analysis and concept formation. To ask this of a child in, say, first grade, however, is to require a task that ultimately will be frustrating.

The development of the capacity to reason and classify occurs in a specific order, and it does the child a gross error to try to override that order. If you ask a five-year-old to think like a child of eight (even though he may possess the vocabulary), he will have trouble. And if a child often is faced with this frustration, he will begin to think of himself as a failure.

A lack of progression in learning is a warning sign to you. For instance, if your child isn't a better reader at nine than he was at eight, this is generally cause for concern. If he's not more coordinated, if he's generally not developing, these are also warning signs. You must, however, focus on *normal* progression, whether your child is progressing at the same rate as other children, *not that he is excelling*. Too many parents look for their child to excel and misdiagnose normal development for slow development. You should not expect a two- or three-year-old to be very social or to be good at sharing. But a child of five should know what sharing means and should show some interest in doing so.

DANGER SIGNALS: WHEN TO SEEK PROFESSIONAL HELP

As we indicated at the beginning of this discussion, a child who is severely disturbed by being rushed will display extreme forms of behavior indicative of children who grow up too fast. There are certain other indications, however, that if present in any form, should warn you that your child is in acute distress and may require professional help. As in all our recommendations regarding childhood problems, it is best to err on the side of too much instead of too little. If you suspect any major difficulties with your child, seek professional help. You may want to speak with your child's teacher, pediatrician, or other adults with whom he is in contact. They will usually have had experience with this or similar problems and will be able to help you assess your concern. This is one place where you should not be afraid to rush, however. Your child has only so much time, and your job is to help him make the most of it.

• *Abnormal eating habits*—Although studies increasingly indicate that a tendency to be overweight is hereditary, some children overeat as a way of nurturing themselves. Overeating provides a means of compensating for feelings of emotional deprivation. Such a child usually is not one who's been chubby all his life, but has suddenly changed his eating patterns. A child who's eating constantly may be at risk of developing severe emotional problems. Conversely, a child who's stopped eating and shows no pleasure in food may also be at risk and need professional help.

 • *Acting out*—Children act out their emotions for a variety of reasons. Two causes you can anticipate are depression and anxiety. The child wants attention from you, his teachers, and his peers, and he also may need a way to rid himself of some of the tension he's feeling. If your child is getting in trouble in school regularly, if you catch him lying excessively, or if he constantly throws tantrums or seems to be out of control, he may be at risk. These children often show little respect for authority figures and frequent negative reports from your child's school are a warning sign. In such cases, you should have a complete and thorough discussion with your child's teacher before determining whether or not professional help is required.

 • *Lying and stealing*—It's not necessarily a terrible sign if your young child occasionally "takes" something. But if your eight- or nine-year-old regularly steals from other children at school or from a parent's purse, or if he steals something of significance, it's a sign of a serious problem. Marilyn, for example, is a ten-year-old gifted child who was very unpopular at school. In an attempt to establish esteem with her peers, she told the other children in her class that her father was the president of the company that made Garbage Pail Kids. She claimed she had the whole set of Garbage Pail Kids cards, Series one—a very valuable collection. When her friends didn't believe her and dared her to bring the collection to school, Marilyn actually stole the cards from a neighbor.

● *Lack of friends*—A child who eats alone and plays alone is letting you know that something's very wrong. He is showing you he's not social; perhaps he's not well liked or doesn't know how to interact with other children. If you suspect this is the case with your child, you should check with his teacher and with the staff of his pre- or after-school facility. As we indicated previously, you should be acutely sensitive to your child's interaction with other children.

● *Excessive trouble with separation*—Sandra is a seven-year-old child who constantly needs to be in the physical presence of her parents. She won't even go into another room unless accompanied by her mother or father. If your child is older than six or seven, he should have passed the stage of separation problems, and any child who displays this kind of behavior may need professional attention. The desire in a child to not grow up may be a result of feeling pressure to grow up too fast.

● *Difficulties with sleeping*—A child who has a chronic and prolonged problem sleeping or has frequent nightmares needs help. All children experience problems sleeping at one time or another, especially after such traumatic events as seeing a scary movie, listening to a spooky story, or having a favorite pet die. However, a child with frequent sleep problems may need to have an evaluation by a professional.

● *Lack of friendship skills*—Lack of friendships has a number of causes, and it may be temporary. But if it's chronic and seems to be related to a lack of friendship *skills*, the problem will eventually become severe and will initiate a negative cycle. A child who perceives himself as unlikable will eventually find himself suffering from a deflated sense of self-esteem. This child looks around class and sees other students relating to each other while he is all alone. This takes a notch out of his self-esteem. When all the children are invited to a birthday party except him . . . .

● *Self-deprecation and melancholy*—The child who constantly says, "I'm so stupid; I can't do anything right. I wish I wasn't born. You'd be happier without me" is at risk. Given the increased rate of teen suicide, you should take a child seriously when he says something like that. Therapists see depression in children as young as two or three. The child who doesn't seem happy, who feels he has no influence on his environment, or who feels unable to please anyone is suffering. Although you may see this kind of melancholy in younger children, it's important to know that the older the child, the more there is concern about suicide. Also remember that a disturbed child may hide his problems with headaches, stomachaches, or other forms of behavior.

● *Excessive noncompliance*—A child who won't do anything anyone asks of him may need help.

Often children act this way because they feel a strong need to control their world. We might expect noncompliance in a three- or four-year-old. As a child gets older, however, we expect him to comply with such rules of the game as coming home at the required time, calling when he's going to be late, and obeying the rules of interaction with other family members. Again it is a question of degree. A child who says no a lot is not necessarily a problem, but a child who is chronically noncompliant in almost every area in which demands are made of him—a child who refuses to wear his seat belt, who refuses to pay attention to any rules or expectations of his behavior—is a child in trouble. The same is true of a child who is mean to other children or to animals, who is liable to say terrible things when he's angry, who doesn't seem capable of being "nice."

The types of children described here may indeed be in need of professional care. Be mindful, however, there is much you can do alone and in conjunction with a therapist. The following part tells you what and how.

Part III
Slowing Down, or How to Help Your Child Make the Most of Childhood

We have discussed a number of reasons why your child might want to grow up too fast; we also have provided you with some guidelines for determining whether the problems you see in your child result from being pushed too far too fast by himself or by others. Now we come to how you can help prevent this from happening. Although our emphasis is on prevention, you will also find some suggestions for taking care of situations that may have already become a pattern in your family life.

You may have discovered yourself and your own actions in these pages. You may have realized that because of social pressures and the demands of your own life, you inadvertently have been asking too much of your child—and, perhaps coincidentally, been giving too little. Although it may at first be frustrating to think of reevaluating your expectations and examining your views of child rearing, be advised that this is not as difficult as it might seem. Life, after all, is a process of constant growth and development, for you and your children.

The information presented here suggests ways you can restructure your life with your child to make it easier for him . . . and for you. Although children suffer considerably from being rushed through childhood, you also have a host of difficulties and frustrations you must confront: disappointment when your child doesn't do as well as you think he should, anxiety and concern over a child who seems to be unhappy and failing in life, and most of all, frustration at not knowing how to help him. Your children provide the focus of your life in many ways; if they are unhappy, there is no way you will find peace and contentment.

We all have dreams of what childhood should be like, fairy tales perhaps. Reality has a way of intruding on these dreams, and life is always more difficult than we would like. Once that fact is acknowledged, however, it is infinitely easier to move forward, identifying and confronting difficulties. It is the parent or child who attempts to proceed with an unrealistic idea of what life will demand of him who continually is surprised by its challenges and unprepared to meet them.

There are currently no studies indicating that early learning is an advantage for a child. Children who progress according to normal developmental standards and are not pushed forward eventually make as much progress as those who are intensely encouraged. Children who learned to read in kindergarten, for example, show no better reading results than those who started to read later. The downside of accelerated learning is that pushing a child in school or otherwise can lead to unnecessary, nonproductive stress. Children, strange as it may seem, can actually "burn out." Like adults exposed to overly intense experiences over a period of time, burned-out children simply give up. They don't *want* to go to school; they don't *want* to try. They develop chronic illnesses; they become depressed and stressed. These unfortunate children have lost the sparkle of childhood. And it can happen as early as third and fourth grade, sometimes even before they're in kindergarten.

So be a wise parent. *Help your child to be a child.* Help your child build a strong foundation in childhood that will stand him in good stead for the rest of his life. If you invest too much in being proud of him when he's young, you might find that you and your child will have to face severe problems with failure as he reaches adulthood. Then the stakes will be much higher and the chance of recovery less. Not all of the following suggestions will apply to you or your child. Nonetheless, take time to study them carefully, along with the examples provided. You'll find that life for you and your child will become much more pleasant.

We have seen that there are a number of factors that induce parents to rush their children through childhood. These include the parent's desire to have the child measure up to or compensate for the parent's level of achievement, as well as the parent's susceptibility to social standards of success. There are different ways you can reverse established patterns, right wrongs, and prevent problems from happening. As with any child or adult, it is preferable to prevent a problem's occurrence than to remedy it once it has appeared.

THE TERRIBLE NEGATIVE EFFECTS OF GROWING UP TOO FAST

Therapists are all too aware of the problems experienced by a child who is encouraged to be competent beyond his years and who is conditioned to want to act in ways that are inappropriate for his age and capabilities. If your child shows any signs of the following, you should stop and think about how he's growing and maturing.

Bad Feelings About Being a Child

When a parent, teacher, or any other adult expects more of a child than what he is capable of, the child's typical response is anxiety. A five-year-old child may respond to his parents' desire to have him sit through a meal at a fancy restaurant. But at what price? Fear, certainly. Anxiety. Most of all, asking a five-year-old to do this kind of thing makes the child feel bad about being a child—because he doesn't really want to do what his parents want him to do. The problem is he loves his parents and wants to please them. *Parents need to assess their own motivation* in such circumstances. Are they perhaps trying to show the child off? Will the child's good behavior reflect on you as parents? Better that the child eat a quiet meal at home and leave the Cordon Bleu to the adults. (Chances are, he won't like the food anyhow.)

This problem is often the most acute in the area of education, where parents invest heavily in their children's ability to excel. Perhaps we should take an example from Sweden, where children don't start school until age seven. The Swedes report a tremendous reduction in learning disabilities compared to the problems our children experience in this country. Are their children any more intelligent than ours? It would be difficult to believe so. The Swedish culture simply has a different sense of when children are ready to learn (and compete).

When parents put pressure on their child to learn to achieve beyond his limits, it has serious repercussions for their relationship. The message the parents have to convey to the child is, "You're not OK the way you are, but you can make me feel better about you (and about me), if you're an intelligent child—which you can demonstrate by reading early, by excelling in mathematics, by being the best speller on the spelling team."

Negative—"Don't Be"—Messages

Children urged to mature too quickly are often the recipients of many "don't be" messages—don't be silly, don't be a goof-off, don't be inattentive. What it all adds up to, of course, is: *Don't be a child.* Anytime a child receives one of these "don't be" messages (which are, by their nature, negative), it decreases his sense of self-esteem and worth. It makes the child feel that he is valued only for what he can do, not for who he is.

Turning Children Inside Out

Many experts are concluding that children who are in a rush to grow up too fast are often so overexposed to stimuli at very early ages that later they become easily bored. Such children become occupied with a constant search to keep themselves entertained. Parents who expose their child to too much—games, toys, and activities—will find that the child never expresses an intense desire for anything, whether it be to *have* something or *do* something. Often such an overstimulated child actually suffers from a lack of imagination. He has little ability to live inside himself, and constantly searches for stimulation from the outside world. Later this burned-out child is exactly the one who will be drawn to the excitement of drugs, antisocial behavior, or premature sex in an attempt to duplicate the level of sensory thrills and excitement he has been conditioned to since childhood.

Overstimulated children—from toddlers to teenagers—can't entertain themselves. Giving an infant a toy or game to keep him occupied and out of our hair will become something far more dangerous as the child gets older. As the child grows, the toys become more and more expensive and more valuable—cameras, computers, a VCR. The end effect is that these "gifts" inhibit the child from creating his own entertainment. He will come to expect someone else to amuse him, to stimulate him. And he may become desperately afraid of being alone, faced with the prospect of amusing himself.

Destructive Adolescent Behavior

One of the characteristics we often see in adolescents in contemporary society is an abrupt closing of the family door—literally and figuratively. In the tight nuclear family, we have come to accept and allow less communication between children and parents. Children insist on privacy, shunning questions about school and their social life, which they feel are intrusive. Angry teenagers often employ the technique of putting down family values. Such children often display a great interest in the opposite sex.

This behavior is disturbing enough in teenagers, but when children of ten and eleven begin acting like adolescents, it should truly be cause for alarm. These children pull away from their parents, often displaying the rage and capricious emotional reactions that we are more used to in teenagers. Confused parents often allow this to happen because they see no alternative. It is almost as if they have created a monster that they can't control. Therapists and counselors are not surprised to hear that young adolescents whose family regulations are lax are regularly engaging in sexual intercourse. Often parents of these children find it difficult to enforce curfews and are strangely blasé about not knowing where their child is. In many cases, this laissez-faire attitude comes from the parents' fear of fighting with their children.

WHAT TO DO

Using the following techniques can help you prevent the problems that may arise when your child grows up too fast by helping you to be aware of the pressures your child may be feeling and to reduce their effects.

HELPFUL HINT #1—KNOW YOUR CHILD

As a parent, your first task is to *observe*, not push, your child. Take cues from his skills, interests, and reactions to circumstances and the behavior of others. If you have doubts about how your child should act in certain situations at a certain age, speak with other parents, with his teachers, and with the staff at his aftercare center. This is particularly important if you're a working parent or single parent. Often the time you are able to spend with your child is limited, so you must make sure that what time you do spend is *quality time*, when you can give undivided attention. Speak with those adults who regularly come in contact with your child to see whether they notice that he has any problems or is acting differently from other children his age.

This is crucial when it comes to establishing the amount of care-taking behavior a child is capable of at a given age. Remember, wanting your child to assume a certain level of responsibility because it will make your life easier doesn't mean that he is capable of it.

HELPFUL HINT #2—GOOD PARENTS ALLOW THEIR CHILD TO STRUGGLE

Parents who are truly interested in life-long progress for their child will *encourage rather than exhort*. They will take their direction from the child.

Encourage your child, but don't do his work for him. Often parents become impatient with children who are not working up to the parents' standards. Before you get out the crayons and pencils, however, think about whether your standards are realistic. Do they really relate to your child, or is it *your* ambition showing? Are *you* competing with the child down the block or at the head of the class? Remember, there is a direct relationship between how much you do for a child and how good or bad he may come to feel about himself.

Good parents allow their children to struggle and praise them when they succeed. These parents go out of their way to find things their child does well so they can reinforce him when he does a good job. From this, he will begin to feel good about himself. Spend time talking with your child in a way that he understands, in terms and values that have meaning in his life. Forget the designer jeans; they only have meaning if you suggest it. Think about things that are important to his life: how he throws a ball or whether he can answer a question correctly in class.

HELPFUL HINT #3—RECOGNIZE "TEACHABLE MOMENTS"

As a busy parent, sometimes your best opportunities for quality time with your children are informal, spontaneous moments. This may be in the car on the way to the supermarket or when you're putting your child to bed, when he says something that sparks the opportunity to teach a value or discuss a problem. Often these are far more successful times for communication than a formal parent-child conference. When a child accompanies you to the store and sees you buy the middle-priced pair of slacks, and you explain you're going to use the slacks to work in the garden, you have taken advantage of a teachable moment. It's one of the great rewards of raising children that special moments between you and your child can happen unpredictably. It's your special chance to be there, and to be willing to enjoy using these moments to help your child grow.

HELPFUL HINT #4—HELP YOUR CHILD SOLVE HIS PROBLEMS; DON'T DO IT FOR HIM

Once you have established a line of communication with your child, you can encourage him to talk about the things that are bothering him. *Help your child find better solutions to his difficulties; don't solve the problems for him.* Remind him that everyone has difficulties and everyone will make mistakes; the most rewarding thing is to *try*.

It's important that you learn to distinguish between a real and an imagined problem. Louise, for example, continually complained about her second-grade teacher. The subject invariably came up just before she went to bed. For more than a week, her mother ignored Louise's complaints, thinking that the child was just having a personality conflict with the teacher. When Louise mentioned that a friend down the street and a few of the other children were also upset about the teacher, Louise's mother decided to investigate. After talking to other parents, she discovered Louise's teacher was giving the children assignments requiring so much work that the children had no time to do anything else. The parents got together, reviewed the assignments, and concluded that the children's complaints were justified. They requested a meeting with the teacher to express their concerns. They explained that the children were stressed and unhappy. The teacher was new to the school and was trying to impress her principal. Although it took her a while to admit that the children were being given too much work, she eventually agreed to scale down their assignments.

In an individual case where you disagree with the teacher's handling of your child, you should first allow your child the chance to work it out with his teacher. But if you think your child is excessively stressed, you may need to step in and help. You can explain to the child your concerns and your plans to do something about it. Then you should meet with the teacher or ask for help from a school resource specialist or principal. When you approach the teacher, you should explain that your interest is in solving the problem *together.* Your child may not be able to change teachers, and he has to learn—with you—how to handle the situation.

HELPFUL HINT #5—BE YOUR OWN PERSON

Often parents give in to pressure when their child comes to them and says, Johnny's doing it, why can't I?" (And Johnny often is an older child.) No one doubts that in the short run it's easier to give in when your child attempts to manipulate you this way. You can justify it by saying it will make the child feel better, will make you feel "cool," and will give you a sense of well-being as a parent. In the long run, however, you will know when you did the wrong thing by allowing the child to talk you into something. If you have questions, or if you wonder how much of what a child is saying is the truth, it's easy enough to consult other parents. Whether the issue is allowance, proper bedtime, what movies your child can see, curfew time, even what clothes the other kids are wearing, check with other parents. Remember, a happy child is one that knows his limits, so don't issue edicts prematurely. Think the situation over, then lay down the law simply and firmly—and stick to it.

In investigating what is normal for your child's age, don't limit yourself to your child's friends. Talk to the parents of the boy down the block who goes to another school. Sometimes a teacher is a good source, and it doesn't necessarily have to be your child's teacher; sometimes it's better to get a second opinion. Talk with your own friends who have children the same age.

When you set limits of any kind, try not to be arbitrary. Assess your child's needs. Take, for example, the matter of allowance. Discuss with your child his idea of his expenses, and feel free to negotiate with him. Remember also that a child's needs fluctuate depending on events at school, time of year, and other variables. Forcing your child to think through this process is far more nurturing than the easier way of picking a ballpark figure. A child needs to be able to handle the amount of money you give him, so you will have to take this into consideration also. Additionally, it's important for you to establish an incentive system for your child. The two of you may agree on a certain weekly amount, even though it's not what the child asked for, and *you* know that it's not enough. You can then suggest that he supplement this by doing extra chores around the house or yard. This is a very effective way of showing cause and effect; when your child wants such extras as a new toy or special piece of clothing or book, he will understand he must work for these luxuries.

There will, of course, be times when it will be impossible for a child to raise all the money he needs for something special, and he will still need supplemental income from you. Most families establish an annual or semiannual budget for such things, but children excel at coming up with the unanticipated. Get set on your strategies for dealing with these situations, and stick with them. Again, don't be arbitrary; try to make it a learning experience for your child. Let's look, for example, at Josh's conversation with his father about a skateboard he wants to buy. Like most children his age, seven-year-old Josh knows which brands of skateboards are the best and which one he wants; it happens to be the one that twelve-year-old Mike has.

Josh: *Daddy, I really need a skateboard. All the other kids have them, and I don't. Please, can I have one?*

Dad: *I don't know, Josh. Tell me about it.*

Josh: *Mike, my friend next door, has an AWA board, and they're the best. They've got all the good stuff on them. They're really neat.*

Dad: *How much are these skateboards?*

Josh: *About $100.*

Dad: *One hundred dollars! That's a lot of money.*

Josh: *I know, but they're the best.*

Dad: *I thought you could get one for $35.*

Josh: *You can, but those aren't any good. I need one of the really good ones.*

Josh is asking to be treated like an older child. After talking further, it turned out that Mike has been a skateboarder for years and really needs a good board because he competes in skateboarding exhibitions. Josh, however, is a rank beginner. His father argues, and rightfully so, that Josh has no need for the more expensive board, which is also beyond his ability to use. By not being arbitrary and by holding out the possibility that if Josh becomes good at the sport he'll get the expensive board, Josh's father will be motivating the child to work toward a goal. It's quite possible that if he gives in and provides the money for a more expensive model, Josh might not be able to handle it. Frustrated, Josh might give up the sport before he even starts.

Here is what Josh's father finally decides:

Dad: *Josh, Mike is twelve years old and had a different skateboard for many years before he got the AWA. You're not as old as Mike, and you're not as good a skateboarder because you're just starting. I'm sure with a lot of practice, you'll be good, and then, when you're older, we can talk about getting you a better board. For now, I'm not willing to get you the most expensive one.*

It took a couple of days for Josh to accept his father's decision, but he eventually bought the $35 board and has been enjoying taking lessons from Mike. It's too soon to know whether he will ever justify getting the more expensive model.

HELPFUL HINT #6—DON'T FORCE YOUR GOALS OF PROGRESS ON YOUR CHILD

There are two subtle vehicles by which parents frequently communicate to children what their goals for them are. First and more obvious are the gifts they give their children; second is the playtime behavior they expect of their children. Although most toys are marked with the recommended age for which they are suitable, many parents buy toys that are designed for older children. This conveys the subtle message we spoke about earlier—"I want you to do more than you're doing now."

You can rectify this situation by having a talk with your child and simply saying, "Your father and I have noticed that most of your toys are really designed for kids of eleven, which is three years older than you are now. I think you might have more fun if we picked out some things that are more suitable to your age. Let's go to the store and do it right now. Maybe someone there can help us."

Some parents become extremely anxious when they discover their child has a favorite toy that is for a younger child—a toy he may have had for years and doesn't want to give up. More often this is more of an emotional attachment rather than lack of intellectual development, and parents are wise to see it that way. Candy Land, for example, is known as a child's "first game" because it's simple. Although it's recommended for young children, many ten- and eleven-year-olds love to play it. One eleven-year-old admitted to a friend's parents, "Gee, if my dad saw me do this, he'd kill me. It's a baby game." The truth is that older children frequently like to play games that are designed for younger children because they know they have expertise at them.

As we've noted, development isn't a constant forward process; adults know that even about themselves. Some days it's easier to drop back into behavior we thought we'd gotten rid of. Likewise, you need to allow this of your child sometimes. Playing a game he's good at, even though it may be "too easy," can be an enormous confidence-builder for your child. The same thing applies to movies, television, books, and magazines. A child may have a favorite story or "silly" TV program. To deprive him is not only to take away some joy from his life, but also to make him feel bad about his enjoyment.

You should, however, stick to the rules. Take the example of Sally, who is nine "going on nineteen." She is popular at school and has a very active social life. She spends a lot of time talking with girlfriends about boys and the latest clothes and hairstyles. Like some of her friends, Sally enjoys acting "grown-up" and actively pursues activities that will help her reach beyond her years. She buys adult fashion magazines, window-shops in the teen clothes section in department stores, and likes to watch "grown-up" shows on TV. Her mother is concerned about Sally's preoccupation with being grown-up and has decided to try to do something about it. The first thing she tackled was TV. This is how Sally's mother approached the problem one evening when Sally was getting ready to watch a favorite program:

Sally: *Mommy, can I stay up tonight to watch my favorite show?*

Mom: *No, Sally, you have a big day tomorrow and a test. I'd like you to be in bed at a reasonable hour.*

Sally: *Oh, c'mon, Mom, I already studied for my test, and besides, all of my friends are staying up to watch the show. [This is the childhood lament heard around the world. It means, "C'mon, everybody else will get to stay up if you go along with it, because you'll be the first."]*

Mom: *No, Sally, I don't think so. I've been thinking that you're not getting enough rest for a child of your age. I checked with a number of your girlfriends' parents, who've told me that bedtime in their house is nine o'clock. So I've decided that until you're older, you should be in bed by nine.*

Sally: *Oh, Mom, you always do this to me. You treat me like such a baby, and you just don't realize that things are different today. I'll go to bed right after my show.*

Mom: *No, Sally. There's no discussion about this. I've thought about it a lot. And bedtime is nine o'clock.*

Sally: *Mom, I promise. Lights out as soon as the show is over.*

Mom: *No, Sally, I've made up my mind. When you*

get older, then you can stay up later, but for now, you'll be in bed at nine.

Although Sally did her best to manipulate her, Sally's mother took the one step that her daughter couldn't get around. She talked to other parents and discovered Sally was the only one who was allowed to stay up late on school nights. Children's strategy in situations like this is simple: they think that if they annoy you long enough, you'll eventually give in. And many parents, out of fatigue or frustration, do just that. In this case, however, Sally's mother thought about the issue carefully, knew her own limits, and ended the discussion.

HELPFUL HINT #7—PROVIDE GOOD EXAMPLES

You are a prime source of modeling for your child. Too often, parents forget that. But various studies on reading, for example, have shown that children raised in homes where the parent reads the newspaper, magazines, or the latest bestseller will be more likely to read than children raised in households where the TV is always on and little reading material is available. If you're always watching television but expect your child to read, you're bucking the odds. It's probably not going to happen. But if your child is exposed to books at home, if you read to him, there's a good chance he will come to enjoy reading. This will help motivate him when it comes time for him to learn to read in school. Remember, however, that the fact your home is full of art or classical music or good books is not a surefire guarantee that your child will develop a similar interest or that he will do so at the age you think is appropriate. But the fact your home is full of enrichment opportunities will give him a head start. The idea is to provide a casual introduction, not a structured program.

Because a child's sociability is so important to healthy development, you should try to provide a model of being a good friend. A young child often will come to his parents and ask them to arbitrate a dispute with another child, or ask their opinion of an action he has already taken. Often this is an attempt to justify his actions, but on occasion he actually wants genuine input. This is another one of life's little opportunities to teach, and you should take advantage of it.

Let's say Billy just lost a couple of his special Garbage Pail Kids cards. His friend Jerome goes up to him and says, "Here, I have some extras; why don't you take some of mine?" Billy, a little overwhelmed by the gesture, accepts, and Jerome goes home and tells his parents what he has done. His parents might have a number of responses. One would be for his mother to say, "You know, Jerome, that shows me you're a nice boy. You were able to go up to someone who didn't feel very good and share something of yours. That's a wonderful thing to do. That shows me you're a good person inside." Another parent, however, might say, "Jerome, that was silly. I worked hard for that money. I bought you those Garbage Pail

Kids, and you don't just go around giving things away. Not just that; Billy's father makes more money than I do, and he can afford to buy his own cards. You're a fool for doing that."

The two responses convey two very different messages about the same experience. The first response teaches Jerome the value of friendship and of recognizing how other people feel. The second response is negative and primes Jerome to value money and possessions. If the second response is typical of what your child hears at home, he will eventually experience problems with sociability. He may come to be seen as stingy and will not be well liked, despite his own inclinations as a warm and sharing individual. It may not seem important, but sometimes parents say things to children without thinking, out of frustration. You need to be constantly on the watch for that.

HELPFUL HINT #8—HELP YOUR CHILD IDENTIFY FEELINGS

It's extremely reinforcing when you help your child identify his feelings. When your child comes in and says, "I don't want to play anymore with Jerry and Ira," you can respond in a number of ways. One response could be, "Good, they don't deserve to play with you. You're too good for them." (In this case, it may be that the parent is personally offended more than he or she is concerned about the child.)

Another, more helpful response would be, "Well, Richie, it seems like you're really angry and upset. Can you tell me about what you're feeling? What happened?"

With that kind of statement, you have opened the door for discussion. More importantly, you have encouraged your child to talk about his feelings, conveying an equally important but subtle message that it's OK to have feelings and to be hurt or upset in circumstances like this. The next step is for you to discuss ways in which your child can better handle the situation.

Although you may be fearful of doing so, you can talk to your child openly as long as you let him know you care and are concerned. For example, it's OK for you to say to your child, "I know it's really hard for you to be at day-care right after school. I wish I could spend more time with you. What can we do this weekend that would be fun for you?" This recognizes the child's feelings and shows that you care and are willing to extend yourself to make the situation better. Even if he's having fun, and everything seems to be going well, your child wants to spend time with you. It's important to recognize that your child experiences feelings of loss when he is away from you for long periods. In talking to him about this situation, you can also let him know a little of how you feel—that you miss him and would like to spend more time with him.

Be prepared for the fact that the small child, especially, will probably have difficulty understanding *why* you have to be away. He is more likely to think that if it's hard for you, you simply shouldn't continue to do it. Children don't understand the concept of needing to work. Nonetheless, you can attempt to explain, saying something like, "I know you don't understand. It's a grown-up problem, and you probably won't understand until you're a grown-up." The point of the whole conversation, remember, is to encourage the child to talk about his feelings, not for you to launch into a long-winded justification of day-care or your absence.

HELPFUL HINT #9—BE A GOOD, NOT PERFECT, PARENT

Many parents these days have become obsessed with being perfect. This is particularly true of parents who have to be out of the home more than they would like to be. It's a losing game, however, and may have adverse effects on your child. In fact, children seem to thrive when they have parents who try to do *enough* and not too much.

Not only do children benefit when parents try to be average rather than super parents, but parents experience advantages as well. Parents, for example, can accept the fact they're wrong sometimes. They realize they aren't perfect and their children don't need to be perfect either. Being a parent is a difficult job for which we receive little or no training; in fact, most of the training is on the job, and we sometimes make a lot of mistakes.

This I'm-less-than-perfect attitude allows you the luxury of being human. You realize that after a full day of work, and with a full briefcase, there will be nights when you trudge home tired. You acknowledge that if your child pulls at you or demands attention, sometimes you may blow it and yell at him, completely forgetting your goal of quality time and all your other good intentions. Such an attitude allows you to accept that this kind of thing will happen from time to time and helps you say to your child later (when you've recovered and gotten things in order), "I'm sorry I blew up. But tomorrow the pressure will be off, and we can spend some time together."

This perspective allows you to speak with your children about the mistakes you've made and not feel terribly guilty and burdened about them. It also demonstrates to your child that everyone makes mistakes; mistakes are part of life, and *he* shouldn't feel bad when he occasionally "messes up."

Such a parenting style does not call for berating yourself for occasional mistakes. It doesn't require you to feel the need to entertain your child at all times. It even allows that the child may compensate by being bored and finding his own entertainment. It assumes that you will do *enough* to keep your child fulfilled and happy but not *so much* that it robs the child of opportunities for expressing his own personality. It takes for granted that you will provide enough intellectual and physical experiences, but will resist the impulse to be a surrogate teacher (or taskmaster). And most of all, it means you will get to enjoy your child more.

HELPFUL HINT #10—COOPERATE WITH OTHER ADULTS WHO CARE FOR YOUR CHILD

As we indicated earlier, it's very important for you to have contact with the people who have contact with your child: teachers, after-school workers, babysitters. It's not uncommon for alarmed parents to arrive with a child in therapy saying, "I just saw my child's report card, and he's failing math. I had no idea!" Or another parent will be appalled by receiving a notice from aftercare that the child is no longer welcome because he is too aggressive with the other children. This parent also is likely to claim surprise and disbelief.

Not only is it important to discuss with the other adults who care for your child what their observations are, but you must also be prepared to take an adversary role if you discover a situation you're unhappy with. Your child may be unable to come to aftercare following a full day of school and do his homework. He may be the kind who needs to play for an hour or so and then do his work. That's information that you need to communicate to the aftercare staff.

It's important to provide feedback about your child. You should be able to say, for example, "My child is not a worker; he won't sit in a group and do his homework. So could you check him to be sure he's starting his work?" Or, "My child has trouble organizing. Can you be sure he has a pencil and paper and the materials he needs to do his work?" You can only do this, however, if you yourself are sensitive to your child's needs. And if your preschool or aftercare center won't cooperate with you, you should consider alternative arrangements.

Probably one of the most important things you can do for your children is to establish a good relationship with the other adults who take care of them. Remember to thank them and to let them know you appreciate their efforts. This goes for all the adults with whom your children come in contact: coaches, scout leaders, camp counselors. It's very important to develop good relationships with the people working with your children. Often, parents believe their role occurs in a vacuum, which is simply not true.

HELPFUL HINT #11—ABOVE ALL, LEARN TO CONTROL YOUR OWN ANXIETIES AND EXPECTATIONS OF YOUR CHILD

Enough said!

COPING WITH CRISIS SITUATIONS

Children are very resilient; they can cope with numerous changes if the family deals well with the changes. Moving, changing schools, going to a new camp, or leaving a favorite relative are changes children can adjust to if their parents are aware and talk about the feelings surrounding the events. As children progress through childhood, they will necessarily engage in behavior that demands discipline and strong reactions from their parents. The natural tendency to explore and to interact with his environment may cause a child to break things, to defy parental rules, and perhaps to be aggressive toward other children. This is normal. But a child who is overreactive—crying at the most minor crisis or flying into a rage at his parents whenever he is reprimanded—may need professional help. So, too, with the perfect child. A child who shows *none* of the signs of discipline problems that are part of the normal, healthy process of growing up may not be completing the developmental task required of his age. (For further information, see the companion volume *Creating a Good Self-Image in Your Child.*)

Most kids are not perfect, and you should question a child who seems to need to be so. Why is he so controlled that he doesn't cry or yell? Why is he so anxious about confronting people that he can't say anything bad about anyone? What is this obsession about dressing well, speaking nicely? Such children may frequently lack a tough enough skin to deal with other children who tease them or make demands on them. Therapists worry about the parent who says, "I have the perfect child." It means the child is protected from opportunities to face problems and work through them. . . . And they know there is no such thing as the perfect child.

Lest you become overly concerned about your child, remember that after a life crisis of some sort, you will see signs of backsliding in a child's behavior. If the behavior is associated with a major change in the child's life, it will normally follow three stages over a matter of months: the initial upset, movement toward some good days and some bad days, and then more good days than bad. If your child is getting worse or the symptoms aren't getting *at all* better— if there appears to be a real standstill—then it's the time to have the child evaluated.

EVALUATION AND THERAPY

A good place to start if you have questions about any childhood symptoms is your pediatrician. Explain your concerns, and ask his opinion. If he's unsure about the problem, he'll probably refer you to a therapist. If you feel his recommendations are not in the best interests of your child, be sure to get a second opinion, either from another pediatrician or from a psychologist.

The next step is a psychological evaluation. An evaluation doesn't mean that a child necessarily is committed to therapy, but simply that you and the therapist discuss available options, only one of which might be therapy. Evaluation involves a trained professional speaking with you and other important people in your child's environment (such as teachers, a day-care worker, and other relatives) in an attempt to get an idea of how your child relates to the world. If you are divorced, this would also involve speaking to both sets of parents, stepparents, and other family members. What you want to do is assess how your child is doing intellectually, socially, and emotionally. A trained professional will be familiar with what's normal.

A professional can survey the different aspects of your child's life that may affect his behavior, as well as his skills and level of development. This will take some time, so plan on more than one session. The evaluation may also involve testing your child's learning and social skills. Armed with this information, the therapist will be able to develop a sense of your child as a person and make recommendations. Sometimes what you think of as a behavior problem is really a learning problem. A good evaluation will also consider how your child is doing in relation to his peers and how he learns best.

For example, if a child is acting out because he's bored, or if he's bright but having trouble learning in certain areas, you might want simply to wait and see. The therapist might say, "Things seem to be improving, let's wait a few more months and see if anything else happens." Or the therapist might conclude the child is acting normally and does not need treatment. Another recommendation might be parent training, of which a small amount can be beneficial. Sometimes it may be another member of the family, a sibling perhaps, who needs treatment.

It's important for you to ask questions throughout these procedures. It's legitimate for you to ask how long the process is going to take or to ask about the therapist's orientation and how he plans to work with your child. It's also important to determine the therapist's attitude about confidentiality. For example, does he include you in his sessions with the child? If he discovers something important in the child's life, will he share it? It may be desirable for you to visit more than one therapist. Finding a good therapist is like finding a good pediatrician. Someone who works well for one child may not be compatible with another.

Finally, you should not see therapy as a stigma. We live in a complicated world requiring adaptability to complex relationships. We are not all equally prepared for the challenge, and we lack models of behavior for much of what happens to us. If you don't feel bad about your child's therapy, then chances are he won't. It's essential you communicate to him that this is a positive process and that you support him.

CONCLUSION

If, after all you've read here, to recognize that you've been pushing your child too hard, and if you decide to back off in your effort, your child will experience a tremendous sense of relief. The pressure on your child will diminish, like air out of a balloon. Your whole family will be able to relax. And, as we've said earlier, there's absolutely no need for those problems to continue.

Children are a gift. Treat them well. Wish the best for them, and do your best to help them. Understand that they will make demands on your life. You will best help them by knowing when those demands should be met and when they should be challenged. Most of all, allow your children the opportunity to have their place in the sun; allow them to grow up at the pace that best suits them. Control your anxieties and expectations, and help your children become the best they can be.

In a recent study, researchers were interested to see whether there might be common denominators that would predict professional success. They evaluated scientists, educators, and athletes in an effort to determine whether there were any common factors shared by people at the top of their field, as opposed to people who had not made it to the top. They made several observations:

● None of the people interviewed reported having any inborn talent. The baseball player wasn't the best on the team at age four; the academician wasn't the brightest kid in the class when he was young.

● They had all come from families in which they'd received a tremendous amount of praise.

● They had all asked their parents a lot of questions, which their parents viewed as a chance for their children to learn.

● They had all experienced failure (this was perhaps the greatest distinguishing characteristic), and none of them viewed setbacks as devastating. They saw them as rallying points. They picked themselves up, brushed themselves off, and went on.

Having tried and failed and then tried again is a crucial element in growing up. Unfortunately, we find that it is common among both underindulged children and overindulged children that they aren't allowed to fail and try again. The overindulged child isn't allowed to fail—the adult will do it for him—while the underindulged child doesn't have the positive experience of having an adult talk him through the failure and support him by offering an alternative solution. Neither child has learned one of life's most important lessons: the ability to blunder and work it through. So, if you're determined to provide your child with the best possible opportunities in life, give him the opportunity to fail. It may be the most important gift a caring, *im*perfect parent can give.

Good luck.

REFERENCES

Briggs, Dorothy. *Your Child's Self-Esteem*. New York: Doubleday, 1970.

Elkind, David. *Hurried Child, Growing Up Too Fast and Too Soon*. Reading, MA: Addison-Wesley, 1981.

Musser, Paul, John Conger, and Jerome Kagan. *Child Development and Personality*, fifth edition. New York: Harper and Row, 1979.